PRJC

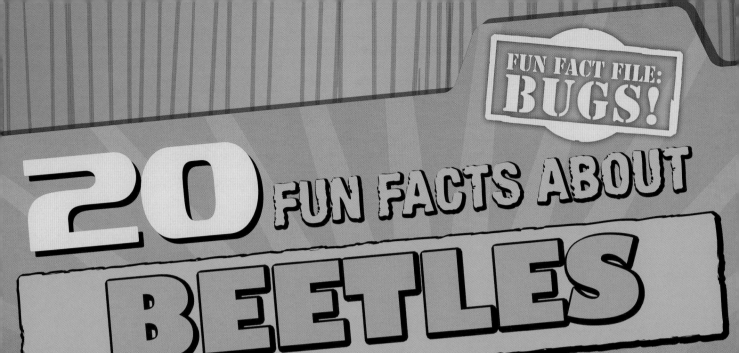

FUN FACT FILE: BUGS!

20 FUN FACTS ABOUT BEETLES

By Arielle Chiger

Please visit our website, www.garethstevens.com. For a free color catalog of all our high-quality books, call toll free 1-800-542-2595 or fax 1-877-542-2596.

Library of Congress Cataloging-in-Publication Data

Chiger, Arielle.
 20 fun facts about beetles / Arielle Chiger.
     p. cm. — (Fun fact file. Bugs!)
 Includes index.
 ISBN 978-1-4339-8226-2 (pbk.)
 ISBN 978-1-4339-8227-9 (6-pack)
 ISBN 978-1-4339-8225-5 (library binding)
 1. Beetles—Juvenile literature. I. Title. II. Title: Twenty fun facts about beetles.
 QL576.2.C45 2013
 595.76—dc23

                              2012020377

First Edition

Published in 2013 by
Gareth Stevens Publishing
111 East 14th Street, Suite 349
New York, NY 10003

Copyright © 2013 Gareth Stevens Publishing

Designer: Ben Gardner
Editor: Greg Roza

Photo credits: Cover, p. 1 Roland Bogush/Flickr/Getty Images; p. 5 watthanachai/Shutterstock.com; p. 6 Paul Aniszewski/Shutterstock.com; pp. 7, 8 Tomas Sereda/Shutterstock.com; p. 9 (larva) Ortodox/Shutterstock.com; p. 9 (beetle) pittaya/Shutterstock.com; p. 10 dexns/Shutterstock.com; p. 11 Nigel Cattlin/Visuals Unlimited/Getty Images; p. 12 Kuttelvaserova/Shutterstock.com; p. 13 Karel Gallas/Shutterstock.com; p. 14 Scott Camazine/Photo Researchers/Getty Images; p. 15 Jackiso/Shutterstock.com; p. 16 Whitney Cranshaw/Colorado State University/Bugwood.org; p. 17 johannviloria/Shutterstock.com; p. 18 Cherice Fuller/Shutterstock.com; p. 19 Jasper_Lensselink_Photography/Shutterstock.com; p. 20 Phaitoon Sutunyawatchai/Shutterstock.com; p. 21 Alex Wild/Visuals Unlimited/Getty Images; p. 22 Petr Malyshev/Shutterstock.com; p. 23 Pengyou91/Shutterstock.com; p. 24 Heiti Paves/Shutterstock.com; p. 25 (green beetle) Henrik Larsson/Shutterstock.com; p. 25 (jewel beetle, bark beetle), 29 Cosmin Manci; p. 25 (goliath beetle) alslutsky/Shutterstock.com; p. 26 Ron Rowan Photography/Shutterstock.com; p. 27 Pavel Mikoska/Shutterstock.com.

Printed in the United States of America

CPSIA compliance information: Batch #CW13GS: For further information contact Gareth Stevens, New York, New York at 1-800-542-2595.

Contents

Words in the glossary appear in **bold** type the first time they are used in the text.

Beetle Creature Features

Beetles have six legs, two feelers, and an **exoskeleton**. These amazing creatures can be very beautiful, helpful, and even entertaining. They also show off many wonderful colors, crazy horns, and odd habits.

Would you believe there are more beetle species, or kinds, than there are species of any other group in the animal kingdom? They make up about 40 percent of the entire insect population. Beetles are definitely one of the strongest and most successful groups of animals on the planet. They've outlived many other animal species—including dinosaurs!

Some beetles look plain, but some are very colorful.

Where in the World?

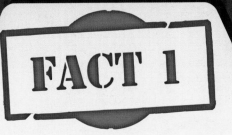

FACT 1

No matter where you go, it's hard to get away from beetles.

Beetles can be found almost everywhere, except in places where it's very cold. They live in freshwater and salt water and on land. Some beetles even survive in hot springs. Many beetles live under the bark of trees both living and dead.

A rhinoceros beetle's horn can be 4 inches (10.2 cm) long.

Beetles have the largest number of species of any animal in the world.

There are over 350,000 species of beetles—more than 1/4 of all animal species. Beetles vary greatly in size and shape. The rhinoceros beetle is the largest. It can grow to 7 inches (18 cm) long. The smallest beetles measure less than 0.04 inch (1 mm) long.

Growing Up Fast

Some beetles live less than a month. Others live for many years.

Some beetles live no more than 3 or 4 weeks. Others can live up to 12 years. Longhorned beetles eat the dry wood in which they live. Since wood isn't very **nutritious**, they spend most of their lives as **larvae**.

Longhorned beetles live between 1 and 3 years. They spend most of that time as larvae.

larva

adult beetle

FACT 4

Adult beetles don't live very long.

Once a beetle completes the process of **metamorphosis** and becomes an adult, its life's journey is just about over. A beetle spends most of its life as a larva. Adult beetles rarely live more than 6 months.

Beetle Body Armor

Beetles have their own suit of armor.

A beetle's hard exoskeleton keeps it safe. It also has two sets of wings. The outer wings, called elytra, are hard. Elytra don't help the beetle fly. They help **protect** the beetle's body. They also protect the soft, inner wings, which are used for flying.

Beetles belong to the animal order Coleoptera (koh-lee-AHP-tuh-ruh). This name comes from the Greek words for "cover" and "wings."

spiracles

Beetle larvae breathe through spiracles along the sides of their body.

Beetles don't breathe through their mouth. They breathe through holes in their armor.

Spiracles are openings along a beetle's body that allow the insect to breathe. Beetles take in air and make pumping movements to force the air throughout their body. The beetles use **muscles** to open and close spiracles so they don't lose too much water.

FACT 7

Beetles use smelly chemicals to find each other.

Beetles can't see very well, so they depend on **chemical** scents to help find each other. Female beetles produce and release scent chemicals called pheromones. Male beetles locate females by following the trail of the scent.

Male scarab beetles use their antennae, or feelers, to follow a female's scent.

Even though beetles communicate by stridulation, people usually can't hear their calls.

To talk to each other, beetles make sounds and vibrations with their body.

Beetles make sounds by scraping their mouthparts together and rubbing their legs together. The process of rubbing body parts together to **communicate** is called stridulation. Beetles that live in a dead log create **vibrations** to communicate with beetles in other parts of the log.

What's for Dinner?

Just about any creature can be a meal for beetles.

Beetles are decomposers. That means they break down and eat many things, including leaves, sticks, grass, dead animals, animal waste, and much more. Almost every product of the animal and plant kingdoms supplies some species of beetle with food.

Carrion beetles work together on decomposing (taking apart and eating) a dead animal. "Carrion" is a dead, rotting animal.

Beetle Battles!

Beetles fight each other for food, sometimes to the death.

Some beetles, such as stag beetles and dung beetles, fight over food. Some even fight until one beetle kills the other. Ladybird beetles, or ladybugs, have been known to lie on their backs and play dead, just like they would if attacked by a **predator**.

Male stag beetles use their large mouthparts to fight and wrestle.

FACT 11

Beetles give off terrible odors when they're in trouble.

When beetles are in danger, some stand on their head and release chemicals from a body part in their rear. The chemicals smell really bad and can turn other animals' skin brown. The horrible smell of the beetle's scent scares off predators.

Some beetles can burn, sting, and bite their predators.

Some beetles have a more painful defense. Bombardier beetles spray a burning, stinging fluid from their **abdomens** with surprisingly good aim. Ladybird beetles, blister beetles, and soldier beetles store defensive chemicals in their blood and release them through their leg joints when attacked.

bombardier beetle

Ding Dung!

FACT 13

Dung beetles make good use of poop.

The dung beetle uses other animals' dung (a fancy word for poop) to eat, lay their eggs in, or even live in. Some dung beetles roll the dung into a ball and move it away for later. Some bury it in underground tunnels.

This group of dung beetles is feeding on a mound of horse dung.

Dung beetles help new trees grow.

When animals eat fruit, the seeds sometimes come out in the animal's waste. Dung beetles move the waste elsewhere and bury it. This puts the seeds safely in the ground. Dung beetles help the **environment** by planting new trees!

Beetles Throughout the Ages

FACT 15

Beetles have been around since the time of the dinosaurs.

The earliest known beetles existed nearly 300 million years ago, along with the dinosaurs. Once plant life started to grow, beetles began to reproduce at an incredibly fast rate, surviving on the food that plants provided.

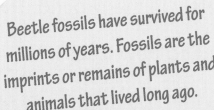

Beetle fossils have survived for millions of years. Fossils are the imprints or remains of plants and animals that lived long ago.

Beetles have outlived many other animal species.

Beetles have been around longer than many other kinds of animals. Their exoskeletons protect them from predators. Flying allows them to escape danger. They can dig holes and even swim, which allows them to survive changes in weather and climate.

Bundles of Beetles

FACT 17

Some people have worn beetles as jewelry.

Beetle colors vary from dull brown to bright greens, blues, and purples. Some are even shiny. Fireflies are beetles that light up the night sky. In Europe and Asia, beetle wings have been used as ornaments for paintings and have even been worn as jewelry.

Beetle colors can be so beautiful that they've been used as decorations by people all over the world. This is a scarab-shaped pin with emeralds.

People around the world eat different types of beetles.

Did you know some people actually eat beetles? Beetles are high in fat and **protein**, which help people survive in places where there's not always enough food to eat. In some Asian countries, adult beetles and even larvae are considered delicious treats!

Name That Beetle!

Many beetles have been named after objects, sounds, movements, places, and other animals. Rhinoceros beetles are named for their large horns. Christmas beetles were named in Australia for their glittery green color and because they suddenly first appeared around Christmastime. How do you think some of the beetles on the next page got their names?

ant beetles	tiger beetle
humpback beetles	
tiger beetles	
monkey beetles	
bark beetles	bark beetle
click beetles	
stick beetles	
fireflies	
carpet beetles	jewel beetle
jewel beetles	
museum beetles	
ladybird beetles	
Christmas beetles	goliath beetle
drugstore beetles	
glowworms	
goliath beetles	

Helpful or Harmful?

FACT 19

Japanese beetles can ruin your garden.

Many beetles feed on the roots, wood, leaves, flowers, and fruit of living plants. Japanese beetles are very pretty, but the adults love to eat green leaves. The larvae love to eat roots. They can be a gardener's worst enemy!

There are about 150 species of ladybird beetles in the United States.

FACT 20

Ladybird beetles can save your garden.

Ladybird beetles, or ladybugs, are interesting to look at, but they're also very helpful. They eat other insects that are pests, such as aphids and mites. However, a few ladybird species are pests themselves because they eat crops.

Beetle Invasion!

The Asian longhorned beetle is an invasive species. That means that it moves into a new area and hurts the local environment. The longhorned beetle eats and destroys many trees. It makes its nest inside piles of firewood. When the firewood is moved or disturbed, the beetles seek out and destroy new trees.

To protect trees and let beetles live in peace, never move firewood from one forest to another. This will stop the beetles from seeking homes in new trees.

The longhorned beetle's "horns" are feelers that can grow to 4 inches (10 cm) long.

Glossary

abdomen: the part of an insect's body that contains the stomach

chemical: matter that can be mixed with other matter to cause changes

communicate: to share ideas and feelings through sounds and motions

environment: the natural world in which a plant or animal lives

exoskeleton: the hard outer covering of an animal's body

larvae: bugs in an early life stage that have a wormlike form. The singular form is "larva."

metamorphosis: the process of change that an insect goes through during its life

muscle: one of the parts of the body that allow movement

nutritious: containing things needed to grow and stay alive

predator: an animal that hunts other animals for food

protect: to keep safe

protein: a nutrient in many types of food that the body uses to grow, repair tissues, and stay healthy

vibration: a rapid movement back and forth

For More Information

Books

Jenkins, Steve. *The Beetle Book*. Boston, MA: Houghton Mifflin Books for Children, 2012.

Prischmann, Deirdre A. *Poop-Eaters: Dung Beetles in the Food Chain*. Mankato, MN: Capstone Press, 2008.

Trueit, Trudi Strain. *Beetles*. New York, NY: Marshall Cavendish, 2013.

Websites

Asian Longhorned Beetle
extension.unh.edu/alb/
Learn more about the Asian longhorned beetle and what you can do to stop it from spreading.

Beetles
www.biokids.umich.edu/critters/Coleoptera/
Read more about beetles and see pictures of them.

Publisher's note to educators and parents: Our editors have carefully reviewed these websites to ensure that they are suitable for students. Many websites change frequently, however, and we cannot guarantee that a site's future contents will continue to meet our high standards of quality and educational value. Be advised that students should be closely supervised whenever they access the Internet.

Index